# SPEECH

OF

# HON. MILTON S. LATHAM,

ON THE

## Pacific Rail Road,

DELIVERED IN THE

SENATE OF THE UNITED STATES,

On the 12th day of June, 1862.

ALSO,

## DEBATE in the SENATE,

ON THE

## Steam Ship Line from California to China,

AND PASSAGE OF THE BILL,

On the 25th day of April, 1862.

---

BALTIMORE...PRINTED BY JOHN MURPHY & CO.

PUBLISHERS, BOOKSELLERS, PRINTERS AND STATIONERS,

MARBLE BUILDING, 182 BALTIMORE STREET,

1862.

# PACIFIC RAIL ROAD BILL.

Mr. LATHAM. I move that all prior orders be suspended, and that the Senate proceed to the consideration of House bill No. 364, being the Pacific railroad bill, which was set down for one o'clock.

The motion of Mr. LATHAM was agreed to; and the Senate, as in Committee of the Whole, resumed the consideration of the bill (H. R. No. 364) to aid in the construction of a railroad and telegraph line from the Missouri river to the Pacific ocean, and to secure to the Government the use of the same for postal, military, and other purposes.

Mr. LATHAM. Mr. President, before the Senate proceeds to a critical analysis of the various sections, I feel it my duty to present a few general ideas upon this important measure, and a special review of the leading features of the bill. I deem this course most economical of the time of every Senator, and perhaps it may obviate the necessity of response to many objections which will legitimately arise in the progress of debate.

The subject of an inter-oceanic railway, uniting the Pacific with the Atlantic, has seriously occupied the attention of the American people and Congress since the admission of California into the Union. There is, in fact, no measure more universally understood and its necessity appreciated by men of all parties, or any more earnestly advocated in years past by distinguished statesmen, than this project now before the Senate of the United States. Mr. Jefferson, at the opening of the present century, saw the importance, nay, necessity, of exploring a route from the valley of the Mississippi to the ocean; at a period, too, when the Republic was in its infancy; its population but five millions; its territorial rights in the vast region within the then Territory of Oregon undefined, the separation of the American from British territorial lines not having been made until nearly forty years after, when adjustment was effected by the Washington treaty of 1846.

The celebrated expedition of Lewis and Clark, through the long, bleak, unbroken wilderness as it was in that age, passing three winters in the enterprise, was more than two years in exploring to the mouth of the Columbia river, having traveled four thousand miles, starting from the confluence of the Mississippi and Missouri, and occupying three years in the overland and return transit.

The time, the toil, the incredible hardships and perils of the expedition show the importance of the contemplated results, destined to affect so vastly the interests of the great American family. Since then, what an amazing change has taken place! Two generations are no more, and the illustrious men of that age have passed into history. The Republic, as it came from the victorious patriots of the Revolution, in virtue of the Declaration of Independence, as recognized in the definite treaty of peace in 1783, fixed the territorial limits in area equal to eight hundred and twenty thousand six hundred and eighty square miles. Those limits, by the Louisiana treaty of 1803, with the French republic, by the Florida treaty of 1819 with Spain, by Texas annexation resolutions of 1845, by the Guadalupe Hidalgo treaty of 1848 with Mexico, and the Gadsden treaty of 1854, have been increased to three millions and a quarter of square miles, double the area of the Roman empire at its greatest period of expansion, after battling for possessions for a thousand years. With its territorial growth has kept pace its population, now thirty-three millions, far advanced in civilization; and by the application of steam as a motive power on land and sea, and lightning as a medium for the transmission of intelligence, the country stands in practical science centuries in advance of any previous era in the history of man. It is not disputed that the progress of the United States in every industrial department has been rapid and constantly sustained,—in agriculture, manufactures, and commerce. The first geographical division, the Atlantic slope, was where these great interests were first developed on this continent.

The restless Anglo-Saxon race, under its new-born Government of freedom, soon spread itself over the great valley of the Mississippi, and now on the Pacific shores confronts the millions of Asia, and is preparing to dispute supremacy with the commercial rivals of the Union. The results of our industrial activity may be understood by a few items of illustration.

The yield of corn alone for the year 1860, was, in bushels, nine hundred millions; the domestic produce exported for the year ending 30th June, 1860, as shown by the report of the Treasury, was considerably upwards of four hundred millions of dollars, and about thirty-eight millions of dollars in excess of foreign imports. To this may be added profits on those exports and cost of transportation in American vessels, all of which it would not be unreasonable to estimate as a gain to our own people in that year's transaction of $100,000,000.

In addition to our foreign commerce, (taking the year 1860 as an average, less than will exist when peace returns,) we have an internal annual trade of over one thousand five hundred millions of dollars carried coastwise, up the bays and large rivers, on the great lakes by steamers and sailing vessels, on the Mississippi and its affluents, by two thousand vessels,—then by overland through the great railway system—a system begun thirty years ago, yet now equal to thirty thousand miles in operation, with sixteen thousand miles additional projected; all together unite in forming a net-work over the older portions of the United States, at a cost of $1,000,000,000.

Now, it is proposed to link these arteries of internal prosperity by *one* which shall traverse the great interior region from the valley of the Mississippi westward to the ocean, uniting with the local system of the Pacific, the land of mineral and agricultural wealth, which, since its admission into the Union, has furnished an annual contribution in gold greater than four times the yield prior to 1850 of the aggregate gold product of the world.

The Congress of the United States, by acts in 1853 and 1854, determined that all question of the feasibility of the measure should be put at rest forever by ordering explorations, which were made in five different latitudes, ranging from our extreme northern limits towards the southern, taking first a direction near the forty-ninth and forty-seventh parallels, then the forty-second and forty-first, the thirty-ninth and thirty-eighth, the thirty-fifth and near the thirty-second.

These elaborate and voluminous details are presented in a series of large folio volumes, published by order of Congress, showing the entire practicability of an efficient route, at different eastern termini, in the wide longitudinal range over a thousand miles, stretching from our northern boundary in the Mississippi valley to the thirty-second degree of latitude.

The condensed tabular exhibit of results which I now present from these railroad exploration publications shows in a clear, methodical, and analytical form, the general direction of the lines of route traversed—air lines, distance by proposed railroad routes, summit of ascents and descents, length of level route of equal working expense, comparative cost of different routes, number of miles of route through arable lands, through regions not equally favorable, the elevation at different distances, and altitude above the sea of the highest points upon the routes.

The eastern half of the Pacific railroad is already a reality, and that upon the most gigantic proportions.

We are now called upon to put an end to delays by coming up to the project with a determination to discard all sectional differences, all questions of unimportant details, and agree at once upon a plan, by legal enactment, which shall secure the construction of this work as speedily as the genius and energy of our artisans can accomplish it. Fortunately, statesmen of all parties agree that there is no constitutional objection, while there can be none of a political or industrial nature. The constitutional power, then, over the subject is complete and undoubted. When Ohio, the oldest of the public land States, was admitted into the Union the General Government was the great land proprietor within the limits of that State. The Cumberland road was projected by the General Government. It cost over six and a half millions of dollars, but its results were immense. The time from Wheeling to Baltimore was shortened from eight to three days, villages everywhere sprang up along the route, and property rapidly advanced in value.

Thirty-four years ago over that road two thousand tons of produce in one thousand wagons were transported from Wheeling to Baltimore, and a stimulus given to intercommunication by turnpikes which awakened into life regions at that time unknown to the quickening influences of trade. It was even then supposed the annual produce taken over the road would be advanced to a hundred thousand tons by cheapening the cost of transportation. Yet, in this principle of cheap transit, the future was destined to produce a revolution incalculable in its results, as found in the inauguration of the railway system.

Congress had, at an early period, exercised the power of appropriating moneys for internal improvements in the States, with their consent. In 1806, an act of Congress authorized a road to be opened from Nashville, in Tennessee, to Natchez. The Cumberland road was made pursuant to a law of that year, under an agreement in 1802 with Ohio that a part of the proceeds of the public lands within that State should be applied to the opening of roads leading to it,—States through which the roads might pass assenting. Other roads were made from Maine to Arkansas and Florida; obstructions in rivers were removed.

Finally, such measures of internal improvement by the General Government were substantially terminated; yet not until after $30,000,000 had been expended, the first serious check to them having been given by President Monroe's veto of the appropriation by Congress of money for repairing the Cumberland road, and establishing gates and tolls. His successor, Mr. John Q. Adams, in his first public State paper as President, favored the exercise of the power by Congress as a constitutional right, and the policy of a liberal appropriation from the public Treasury for works of internal improvement, thereby withdrawing the former weight of presidential authority against that power which Congress had exercised. Afterwards his successor, President Jackson, announced the doctrine that Congress did not possess the authority under the Constitution to appropriate moneys for works of internal improvements of a *local* character, but admitted the power in regard to those of a *national* character.

The State rights doctrine introduced in this respect by the Maysville veto was never denied, but on the contrary, encouraged and justified the exercise of the authority of the General Government in opening military roads and highways over the Territories of the United States, and conferring munificent land grants upon States for railroad communications, stretching from the North to the South, upon a most expanded scale.

This system of land grants, to aid in the construction of railways, began in the State of Illinois by a grant from Congress of an area equal to four thousand and fifty-five square miles, or two millions five hundred and ninety-five thousand acres, twice as large as the State of Delaware. This is called very properly the corner-stone of the great empire system of internal trade and travel. The grant was made to the State of every alternate section, six miles in width on each side of the road and its branches, with an indemnity, where sections were not found, of an equal quantity elsewhere within fifteen miles of the route.

In 1852, the whole line was put under contract, connecting the extreme northern part of the State at Galena to Cairo on the south, with a subsequent branch to Chicago. This main stem was the base of a triangle of which the bend of the river forms the other two sides. The Illinois Central railroad is the longest—four hundred and fifty-odd miles—in the world under any one corporation. Within two years from the date of the grant, ten thousand men were at work upon the line, at an annual expense of $3,700,000. It is now fully equipped, with over one hundred locomotives, one hundred passenger, baggage, and express cars, and also over two thousand freight cars. Already the company has disposed of $16,250,000 worth of their lands, the larger moiety remaining unsold, so that the grant is estimated as equal to $40,000,000 from the General Government to a single State of the Union.

Since then statesmen of the extreme South, as well as North, have given in their adhesion to "land grants" for such great objects; and Congress, by a number of special laws, has made like munificent donations to Missouri, Alabama, Mississippi, Louisiana, Michigan, Arkansas, Florida, Iowa, Wisconsin, and Minnesota, the aggregate being equal to twenty-five millions five hundred thousand acres. The immense, nay, incalculable benefits conferred by these grants within the last ten years, cannot be estimated in the rapid circulation of surplus capital within the great area they embrace.

Now, Senators, look at the condition of our possessions on the Pacific! Are they to be shut out from a participation in the benefits, to gain nothing from the vitalizing influences of these mighty agents of human prosperity—with a sea-line on the western ocean of nine hundred and seventy miles, equal to half the Atlantic; with a population of half a million, which has overcome obstacles and attained results unsurpassed by any State in either hemisphere? When the American flag was first raised in 1846 on those distant shores, the voyage there was a six months' one by way of Cape Horn; then followed the perilous transit over Central America. Soon American energy crossed the Isthmus of Panama with a forty eight mile railway, at a cost of $8,000,000; and lines of steamships on the

Atlantic and Pacific sides went into active operation with a clear profit, for 1860, of nearly $2,000,000. Have we not done our part, with all the toils and privations of pioneers, in fostering on distant shores the institutions of our country—in developing the gold product of our State, which has changed the value of the precious metals and furnished its immense metallic circulation in aid of the commerce of the world--our mines of silver, quicksilver, tin, lead, copper, iron, and coal—our quarries of marble, granite and burr-stone, which are sources of countless profit and wealth to the whole earth? The arable lands of the State were estimated by Captain Wilkes, of the exploring expedition in 1842, at only twelve thousand square miles, or seven millions six hundred and eighty thousand acres. Upon better data, revealed by the progress of settlement, it is since ascertained that the farming lands of the State cover a surface of nearly eighty millions of acres, producing abundance of cereals and fruits of the temperate zone, changing the relation of California from dependence upon importations for bread to that of exporting flour as one of her staples. But the riches of our soil and its various products are known to the Senate and country. To a greater or less extent, exploration and settlement have proved like facts in regard to the agricultural lands of Oregon and Washington—the northern boundary, in part, of the latter being Puget Sound, a great inland sea, destined to have its effect in the trade of the Pacific ocean.

Are these vast interests, in distant localities of the Union, to lanquish and struggle simply because two thousand miles intervene between them and your great Mississippi valley? Is this great interior region still to be traveled the usual laborious way, subjecting the voyager to so many perils, simply for the want of adequate facilities? Have we not a claim to the benefits due by a Government, the theory of which is to confer equal blessings, within its constitutional range, upon every portion of our wide spread territory? The answer to this has been enunciated by the press, in primary assemblies, legislative bodies, representing more than thirty millions of people this side the Rocky mountains, and is now responded to, urged and importunately demanded by the interests of the half million of our citizens west of the Sierra Nevada and Cascades.

Contemplating the interests, which I have so imperfectly suggested of the Atlantic and Mississippi valley on the one hand, and on the other those now existing on the Pacific still to be developed for the benefit of the whole Repulic, present and future, have the representatives of the Pacific not a right to demand your patient, patriotic, prompt consideration and action, upon the important proposition now before the Senate?

The measure before us is clear, comprehensive, and effective in its details, involving no disputed authority. It proposes a railroad system from the Mississippi valley to the Pacific, with a telegraph line. It imposes proper checks and restraints upon the railroad companies—those organized and to be created—to prevent abuses or any improper application of the means placed at their disposal. It gives them freedom in selecting a route, ample time to prosecute and finish the work, and yet is specific in its awards of credits and land grants, exact in securing the interests of the United States by lien in every inch of progress and loan of public credit, and affording reasonable time to all parties. It proposes to lend the credit of the Government by six per cent. bonds, redeemable in thirty years, the loan to be made *pari passu* with the progress of the work, in fixed ratios; and the amount of the responsibility (say $65,000,000) so arranged as to restrict the cost per mile to known and ascertained reasonable valuations; ultimately redeeming the stock thirty years hence, when the mighty results of this work shall have rolled forward to the door of the next generation; thus benefiting the masses at the opening of the next century who will swarm east and west of the Rocky Mountains and line the Pacific shores. The roads and branches indicated in this bill make an aggregate of two thousand four hundred and twenty-five miles, which, at the rate of five sections or three thousand two hundred acres per mile, would make the aggregate of the land grant for the Pacific railway only seven million seven hundred and sixty thousand acres.

Now, let us examine this proposed credit and land grant relatively with the territorial extent to be benefited, in contrast with what has already been done by Congress in northern, southern, and middle land States. The geographical surface of the State of Illinois is fifty-five thousand four hundred and ten square miles. The grant to her for railroad purposes, as I have already indicated, is two million five hundred and ninety thousand acres, valued at $42,000,000. The geographical surface of that State, added to the acres of Missouri, Alabama, Mississippi, Louisiana, Michigan, Arkansas, Florida, Iowa, and Minnesota, make the surface of these land States equal to six hundred and eighteen thousand four hundred and one square miles. To these, Congress has donated twenty-five and a half millions of acres in the choicest localities and richest lands, easily converted into farms, in the midst of thick settlements, with fine fields in a state of highest cultivation, with easy and quick access to domestic and foreign markets. The Government having virtually withdrawn as a land proprietor in many of those States, an immense increase value was the consequence to the lands thus conceeded. If, then, we estimate the value of the lands to the ten land States mentioned, at only one half the value of what the Illinois railroad grant is ascertained to be, it will be found to reach the enormous sum of $150,000,000.

Besides all this, Congress by a general law approved 4th of August, 1854, has granted the right "to all rail or plank road or macadamized turnpike company, heretofore, or that may be chartered before the 4th of August, 1862, the right of way over and through any of the public lands of the United States," giving them one hundred feet in width, enlarged to two hundred feet in cases of deep excavation and heavy embankment, with the right to take from the public lands materials of earth, stone, or wood, with the necessary sites for watering places, depots and workshops.

The sum of these amazing results is briefly this, that to ten land States with an aggregate geographical surface of six hundred and eighteen thousand four hundred and one square miles, Congress has granted nearly two hundred millions of dollars' worth of the richest lands, in beautiful localities, on the great highways of domestic and foreign trade.

Now, the States of California, Oregon, and Kansas are together equal to a geographical surface of three hundred and sixty-five thousand five hundred and seventy-three square miles, and the Territories of the United States between the Mississippi and Pacific contain one million two hundred and forty-two thousand three hundred and twelve square miles, equal to the area of thirty States, each of the size of the State of Ohio. The three large States already organized, and the interest of this half-continent territory, representing the dimensions of thirty States, only ask you for seven millions seven hundred thousand acres of wild lands, and the loan of your credit for thirty years, of $65,000,000.

Now, Senators, compare what you have granted to others and what is now asked for us. Look upon that picture, and then upon this! As conscientious, patriotic statesmen—not neglectful of even the least or more distant part of the Republic, every inch of it being confided to your legislative care—moved by the spirit of the imperial Senate of ancient days, never to yield a foot of territory while an enemy was upon it, but constantly guarding its vast outline in all its diversified interest, let me appeal to you to weigh the grave considerations inseparable from this project, and extend to us in justice the benefits of equal laws and equal rights so cheerfully and liberally awarded to other portions of the United States.

It may be said that the existing political commotions, the exigencies of war, and other pressing demands upon the finances of the nation, render it inopportune to add to the pecuniary obligations of the country. Earnestly, vitally important as this measure is to the Pacific States, yet if it could for a moment impair, check, or divert the resources of the Government so as to result in any embarrassment in these times of trial, I answer in the name of my constituents, that they would not now ask it at your hands. They are committed to the support of these institutions, upon the basis of the Constitution, under which the Government of the United States was organized on the 4th of March, 1789, and will stand by it to the last!

Let us, then, inquire if the proposition before us is liable to such exception. The loan of the public credit at six per cent. for thirty years is for $65,000,000, with absolute security by lien, with stipulations by sinking fund from profits for the liquidation of the principal. Official reports and other authoritative data show that the average annual cost, even in times of peace, in transportation of troops, with munitions of war, subsistence, and quartermaster's supplies, may be set down in round numbers at $7,300,000. The interest upon the credit loan of $65,000,000 of bonds will be annually $3,900,000, leaving a net excess of $3,400,000 over the present cost; appealing with great force to the economy of the measure, and showing beyond cavil or controversy that in fact the Government will not have a dime to pay on account of its credit, nor risk a dollar by the act authorizing the construction of this great work. The United States, if there is force in figures, facts, and reason, will secure with a land grant of seven million seven hundred and sixty thousand acres of wild lands, without a farthing's cost, or outlay, or risk, either present or future, a road that will span half a continent, be the great highway of domestic trade, and eventually make the Union the center of the commerce of the world.

*Let it be understood by the Senate and the country that we ask not a tithe for this indispensable work of what has been granted to others for like objects, and that we ask it upon such a basis as will neither in present nor in future draw a dollar from the Treasury.* In fact, such a road would secure the early peopling and development of this vast interior, now comparatively shut in from the world. Along its entire length settlements would immediately form, which it would be the policy and interest of the railroad land grantees to encourage and foster, with the motive of enhancing the value of their own lands, and affording protection to their property.

The line of this great thoroughfare between two oceans, would offer the highest inducements, with every prospect of success in agricultural and mineral regions, now but imperfectly developed. Soon, in fact, this almost blank in our geographical limits would be filled up by industrious producing classes, requiring all the appliances of civilized life. The effect in value upon such public land would be amazing, and the opening up of the arable surface and development of the precious and useful metals; the working of coal mines, the establishment of machinery and workshops, would revolutionize the existing condition of "the plains," filling the waste places with occupation, and preparing the social and political condition of the country for a transition from Territories into sovereign States of the Union, linking by a great federative bond the whole political fabric from ocean to ocean.

The proposition before us is also one of immense importance, looking to the commerce of the East. Advance commercial interests, and you increase the influence and power of the nation. Trade with the Indies was the great desideratum upon the revival of commerce in western Europe. The Italian republics took the lead in the overland commercial intercourse, which virtually ended upon the establishment of Turkish authority in Europe and Africa. The spirit of maritime exploration and rivalry opened by the Portuguese, who more than three and a half centuries ago rounded the Cape of Good Hope, reached the Malabar coast, monoplized the India trade, and placed that inconsiderable kingdom foremost among commercial nations. After the union of Portugal to Spain, the closing of the ports of the Spanish empire to British vessels, the dependence of the latter upon the Dutch for supplies, the revolt of the Netherlands, and the exclusion of the Dutch in their turn from the ports of Lisbon, the European depot of Italian wares, the Dutch, soon followed by the English, sought the direct passage to India, and before the close of the sixteenth century the great East India companies were founded. France, Denmark, and Sweden sought a participation in the trade, but the extraordinary growth of British power in the East, overshadowing all opposition, governed an empire of one hundred and fifty millions of subjects in the East, occupying half the territorial extent of the United States; and having subjected the native princes, with a grasping and remorseless policy rules them with absolute dominion, at a distance from the British metropolis, by the way of Good Hope, of fifteen thousand miles, thus bringing to the British Isles the rich rewards of eastern trade. With all the disadvantages of remote locality from their colonial dependencies, we should take a lesson from the energy of the English in their amazing efforts to overcome time and space in bringing the capitals of Great Britain and the Bengal Presidency into rapid inter-communication. Two different "overland routes," as they are called, are now in operation; the one reaching round the Atlantic, through the Mediterranean sea, to Alexandria, in Egypt—by the Nile, the Isthmus of Suez, and down the Red sea, traversing the Arabian Gulf and Bay of Bengal, to Calcutta; the other, varying only in respect to the transit of Calais and Ostend, through Southern Europe, until the waters of the Mediterranean are reached, and connection formed with the African and Red sea routes.

The demands of British trade are not even satisfied with these facilities, for it is in contemplation to establish a great overland continuous railway from London to Calcutta, starting from Calais, in France, passing through Belgium, Rhemish Prussia, Germany, and Italy, to the Adriatic; thence through Turkey in Europe to Constantinople, down through Turkey in Asia, deflecting towards the mouth of the Orontes, on the eastern shores of the Mediterranean; thence easterly, to strike the Euphrates, down the long valley of that mighty river, passing Babylon, reaching Breporah on the Persian Gulf, skirting the northern shores of the latter;

thence, through Beloochistan, crossing the Indus, and passing over the breast of the Hindoo peninsula, until it shall reach Calcutta—a route of five thousand six hundred miles, bringing the British metropolis and the Bengal Presidency within a week's travel of each other. Grand as is this railway conception, it is but part of the telegraphic line to reach from Falmouth, by the Straits of Gibraltar, to Malta, to Alexandria, in Egypt, crossing the Isthmus down to the Red sea; thence to Kurrachee, on the western side of Hindostan, over the Peninsula to Rangoon, in British India, to Singapore, Hong Kong, Shanghae, in China, Nagasaki, in Japan, and returning to Singapore to connect with the western side of Australia, crossing that continent to the capital of the Province of Victoria, and thence on the existing line to Brisbane, on the shores of the Alpine Australia.

Such are the plans of the commercial power and policy of the British empire, seeking rapid intercommunication by steam, railway, and telegraph with all the great commercial ports of the world, at the public expenditure of hundreds of millions of pounds sterling, and advancing through European, Asiatic, and African territory.

Now, the position the United States occupy on the Pacific ocean in respect to the Indian trade, gives them advantages not possessed by Europeans In point of distance in our Atlantic and European relations, the difference is inconsiderable when the quiet waters of the Pacific are contrasted with the restless and stormy Atlantic. The distance from San Francisco to the southern part of Matsmai or Tesso, the northern Japanese island, being forty one hundred miles; to the southern point of the great Island of Niphon, forty-four hundred and seventy-four miles; to Shanghae, in China, fifty-three hundred and seventy-three miles; and to Honololu, of the Sandwich Islands, twenty one hundred miles. Improvements in marine steam machinery are such that it is not an overestimate to say fifteen miles an hour, in due time, may be attained, and in that event a fortnight would suffice for importations from China, Japan, and other ports.

The exclusive system of Oriental nations has been nearly obliterated by advancing civilization. The British treaty of 1842, at Nankin, restored commercial intercourse to the five ports of Canton, Amoy, Foochoo, Ningpo, and Shanghae. All the benefits of that treaty accrued to us by our treaty with China concluded on 3d July, 1844. After the Chinese war, declared in 1857, there followed the voluminous treaties concluded in June 1858, between China, the United States, Great Britain, and France, by which four additional ports were opened to foreign shipping, and the navigation of the Yan-tse-kiang river made free to all nations. In 1854, the Perry Japanese expedition led to the treaty of opening Simoda and Hakodadi to our vessels; the new treaty of 1857 opened Naugasaki to American trade, and an additional treaty of 1858 still further liberalized the relations between ourselves and Japan. The United States are thus placed where, by reason of geographical position and commercial relations, they possess the means to secure the Asiatic trade, and turn its golden floods towards themselves. All that is now desired to that end is the success of the Pacific steam line to Asia, with a complete connection of California, Oregon, and Washington by the railway now under consideration.

By the completion of this system between New York and Asia, travel from Europe would select as to time and expense the direction across our territory; silks, teas, spices, and other valuable India products would come to us direct, and our eastern merchants and manufacturers be enabled to compete successfully with the trading world, controlling immense commerce and enriching the Republic. The American road over the plains is a little over one third of the proposed overland Indian route, it is all within our own territory, connecting the Pacific sea-coast, which occupies the same relation to Asia as the Atlantic does to Europe. It will be a great medium, imparting wonderful activity to all the industrial interests of the country, and as time is money, through its union with the existing railroads will furnish facilities not merely of domestic trade and exchange, but of easy and cheapened social intercourse between citizens now in remote and distant localities. As a political measure it will guard and secure interests essential to defense from intestine and foreign foes.

1. In the vast region over which this road is to be constructed, hostile tribes of Indians have ravaged and destroyed the property of our frontier men, butchering families of emigrants and settlers, and interrupting even the languid connection which exists between the interior and the seat of Federal power. On this account the Government has necessarily kept mounted and foot-troops for years past, furnishing all their numerous and necessary supplies, and at enormous expense. These hostile tribes roaming on each side of the Rocky mountains from beyond the northern line of the United States down to the Gulf of Mexico, and further on beyond the western basis in California, Oregon, and Washington, the same mysterious, intractable race, slowly vanishing before the white man, require to be held in obedience by material force. Indian wars in these distant portions of our territory have cost the country for years valuable lives and millions of treasure. Besides this, we have now the country laid waste by the Texan enemy with large military force, holding in check and harassing our own small army without the possibility of succor, from the nearest point in Kansas, under several weeks. A road like this would furnish facilities, enabling the military arm of the Government to strike with concentrated force and rapidity, to subdue and repress enemies of the Republic, to protect and guard that exposed and neglected region.

2. The next military aspect of this subject is the exposed condition of the Pacific coast in case of foreign war.

The growth of our commercial power has brought us into superiority over the greatest maritime people of the eastern hemisphere, our tonnage being five millions five hundred thousand, or an excess over them in tonnage of half a million. The popular nature of our institutions is a standing cause of disquiet to the feudal aristocracy of the Old World. Their leading reviews, journals, and parliamentary discussions, breathe a tone almost of animosity toward us, and indicate their yearning hope that this intestine war may end in overthrow and ruin as a great nation. The commercial marine of the United States is found on every sea, visiting the most distant shores, entering every market of the globe, seeking such a division of the rich profits of trade as their energy and enterprise have a right to demand. The sources of British strength and power are to be traced to commerce, which turns toward the seat of empire a deep stream of wealth, fed by affluents from every distant region, and stimulating at home all the industrial elements of that people. We are competitors for a fair division of that trade, and in the ratio in which we lessen her share by increasing our own, we weaken her power, and advance to that position in the family of nations which we feel is the destiny of a great and free people. Between us there is now pending a dispute in regard to the boundary dividing the possessions of the two Powers, involving a question of ownership of San Juan and other islands in the straits of Rosario, in the northwestern angle of the territory of the United States. A recent political event growing out of our belligerent rights has brought to our shores a hostile fleet with all the equipments of war, threatening to strike upon the instant, while a formidable and well appointed army in the Canadas even now keeps watch upon the long line of our lake frontier. We are living in an age when the political elements of the Old and New World are in commotion. A conflict between the principles and policy of the mysterious man who presides over the destinies of France—it may be said, of Europe—and those of the British empire, threatens a crisis by which the United States, as a commercial nation, would be drawn into the vortex. With disturbing causes at home, and threatening relations abroad, are we to remain passive in regard to a measure so essential to our protection; nay, even necessary to the preservation of our territory?

Senators, there is a serious responsibility resting at the door of inaction and delay. Should foreign war come, our western ocean frontier of nearly a thousand miles will be found walled out by the Rocky mountains, the Sierra Nevada, and the Cascades. Months would be required before an army could give relief overland. By sea, Panama, Nicaragua, and Tehuantepec would be closed by hostile fleets, and feeble and ineffectual communication could only be kept up, a distance of seventeen thousand miles, around Cape Horn. We ask not to be dealt with as a broken or dismembered part of this great empire, but that our unity with the eastern half of the American continent be maintained by the means which the nation can so easily command. Our people are true to the cause of the Union; every sympathy, remote as we are from the central authority, is linked to the Government of our fathers, under which we hope to live, and in defense of which we are prepared to die.

Such are the imperious reasons which force me to urge the favourable action of the Senate; and in warning you of the imminent necessity for instant and efficient legislation, it is my duty to solemnly protest that further delay is fraught with perils to the integrity of our territory, and may end in dismemberment and ruin!

Senators, we turn with pleasure from such an eventuality, we hope impossibility, to the contemplation of results, the guarantees for which are to be found in your love of country and devotion to all her interests. In this season of Domestic turbulence we derive satisfaction from the conviction that all attempts at disintegration must necessarily be abortive; that the present is consequently an unatural state of things, from which the deluded portion of our people will recover from the delirium of a fever; that our normal condition is unity; that common language, laws, lineage, blended interests, industrial, social, and political, love of freedom, of representative Government, are moving, controling causes, in fact, the great elements of order and power, which will hush into silence the clashing discord of the hour, and restore the reign of peace and prosperity. Our domestic struggle has not been without its benefits; it has developed new ideas in respect to military and naval strength in the United States, furnishing examples which tell upon the policy and bearing of rival nations. In this struggle a million of men at arms have entered the field, fully equipped with all the modern improvements of war, while capacity exists for the rally of a four-fold number, should necessity require, for the protection of our firesides and altars.

It has further been demonstrated that the pre-existing system of naval defense and attack is entirely inadequate and unreliable. In one maritime war the prowess and skill of our Navy appeared in successful dispute for ocean supremacy. Now we have launched upon the deep, steel clad warriors of such model and power as to mock and defy those "wooden walls" once the boast and glory of proud maritime Powers. The ability of our Government for the rapid construction and multiplication of these new iron engines of naval strength is such as to enable us to place invincible sentinels at the doors of our harbors in the Atlantic, the Gulf, the great Lakes, and in the Pacific.

And when the reign of peace comes, as soon as it must, results will demonstrate the entire competency of this Government to maintain and further, in a spirit of justice, all the varied interests committed to its charge, while the power shall be established and conceded to maintain its extended peaceful and parental rule, from ocean to ocean.

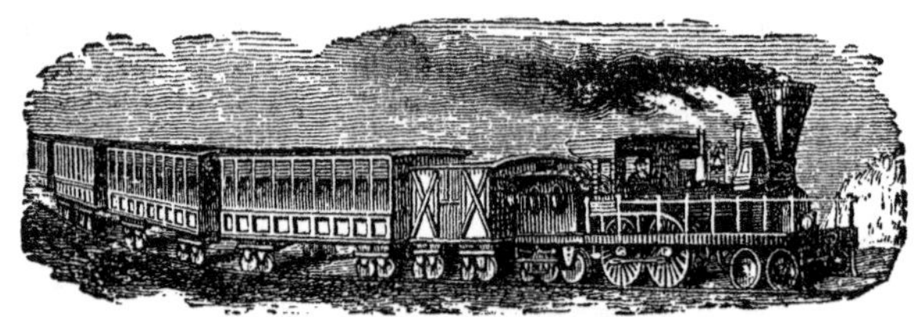

*Table showing the lengths, sums of ascents and descents, equated lengths, cost, &c., of the several routes explored for a railroad from the Mississippi to the Pacific.*

| Routes. | Distance by air line. | Distance by proposed rail-road route. | Sums of ascents and descents. | Length of level route of equal working expense. | Comparative cost of different routes. | Route through arable land. | Route through land generally uncultivable — arable soil being found in small areas. | At an elevation above the sea between— 0 and 1,000 feet. | 1,000 and 2,000 feet. | 2,000 and 3,000 feet. | 3,000 and 4,000 feet. | 4,000 and 5,000 feet. | 5,000 and 6,000 feet. | 6,000 and 7,000 feet. | 7,000 and 8,000 feet. | 8,000 and 9,000 feet. | 9,000 and 10,000 feet. | Altitude above the sea of the highest point on the route | Remarks. |
|---|---|---|---|---|---|---|---|---|---|---|---|---|---|---|---|---|---|---|---|
| | *Miles.* | *Miles.* | *Feet.* | *Miles* | | *Miles* | *Miles.* | *Miles.* | *Miles.* | *Miles.* | *Miles.* | *Miles.* | *Miles.* | *Miles.* | *Miles.* | *Miles.* | *Miles.* | *Feet.* | |
| Route near forty-seventh and forty-ninth parallels, from St. Paul to Seattle | 1,410 | 2,025 | 18,654 | 2,378 | $140,871,000* | 535 | 1,490 | 470 | 580 | 720 | 130 | 97 | 28 | ...... | ...... | ...... | ...... | 6,044 | Tunnel at elevation of 5,219 feet. |
| Route near forty-seventh and forty-ninth parallels, from St. Paul to Vancouver | 1,455 | 1,864 | 17,654 | 2,198 | 130,781,000* | 374 | 1,490 | 309 | 580 | 720 | 130 | 97 | 28 | ...... | ...... | ...... | ...... | 6,044 | Tunnel at elevation of 5,219 feet. |
| Route near forty-first and forty-second parallels, from Councils Bluffs, via South Pass, to Benicia | 1,410 | 2,032 | 29,120 | 2,583 | 116,095,000 | 632 | 1,400 | 220 | 170 | 210 | 160 | 590 | 285 | 270 | 107 | 20 | ...... | 8,373 | |
| Route near thirty-eighth and thirty-ninth parallels, from Westport, via Coo-che-to-pa and Tah-ee-chay-pah Passes to San Francisco.† | 1,740 | 2,080 | 49,985 | 3,026 | Impracticable. | 620 | 1,460 | 340 | 276 | 165 | 348 | 466 | 170 | 60 | 155 | 80 | 20 | 10,032 | Tunnel at elevation of 9,540 feet. |
| Route near thirty-eighth and thirty-ninth parallels, from Westport, via Coo-che-to-pa and Madelin Passes, to Benicia | 1,740 | 2,290 | 56,514 | 3,360 | Impracticable. | 670 | 1,620 | 275 | 308 | 190 | 143 | 725 | 234 | 110 | 155 | 80 | 20 | 10,032 | Tunnel at elevation of 9,540 feet. |
| Route near thirty-fifth parallel, from Fort Smith to San Francisco | 1,550 | 2,096 | 48,521 | 3,015 | 106,000,000 | 646 | 1,450 | 285 | 290 | 261 | 236 | 181 | 295 | 222 | 26 | ...... | ...... | 7,550 | |
| Route near thirty-fifth parallel, from Fort Smith to San Pedro | 1,360 | 1,820 | 48,862 | 2,745 | 92,000,000 | 420 | 1,400 | 354 | 292 | 236 | 210 | 185 | 295 | 222 | 26 | ...... | ...... | 7,550 | Tunnel at elevation of 4,179 feet. |
| Route near thirty-second parallel, from Fulton to San Francisco, by coast route | 1,630 | 2,024 | 38,200 | 2,747 | 90,000,002‡ | 834 | 1,190 | 893 | 347 | 120 | 342 | 271 | 50 | ...... | ...... | ...... | ...... | 5,717 | |
| Route near thirty-second parallel, from Fulton to San Pedro | 1,400 | 1,598 | 30,181 | 2,169 | 68,000,000 | 408 | 1,190 | 478 | 337 | 120 | 342 | 271 | 50 | ...... | ...... | ...... | ...... | 5,717 | |
| Route near thirty-second parallel, from Fulton to San Diego | 1,360 | 1,533 | 33,454 | 2,167 | 68,000,000§ | 374 | 1,159 | 420 | 305 | 125 | 362 | 271 | 50 | ...... | ...... | ...... | ...... | 5,717 | |

* These are the estimates of the office; those of Governor Stevens having been brought to the same standard of increased cost with the other routes, and his equipment reduced to that of the other routes. His estimates were $117,121,000 and $110,091,000.

† Supposing the route to be a straight line, with uniform descent, from the Un-kuk-oo-ap mountains (near Sevier river) to the entrance of the Tah-ee-chay-pah Pass—the most favorable supposition possible.

‡ The estimate of Lieutenant Parke, for the construction of a railroad by this route from Fulton to San José, is $82,812,750. Adding $2,025,000, the office estimate for the route from San José to San Francisco, Lieutenant Parke's total estimate from Fulton to San Francisco would be $84,837,750.

§ The estimate of Lieutenant Parke for this route is $59,005,500.

The sum of the minor undulations (not included in the sum of ascents and descents here given) will probably be greater for the routes near the forty-seventh and forty-ninth parellels than for the other routes. With the amount of work estimated for the roads in this report, the equated lengths, corresponding to the sums of ascents and descents, have but little practicable value. **With a full equipment and heavy freight business, the sum of ascents and descents becomes important.**

# STEAMSHIP COMMUNICATION,

BETWEEN

San Francisco, California, and Shanghae, China,

VIA

SANDWICH ISLANDS and JAPAN.

# Debate in Senate of the United States.

IN SENATE.

FRIDAY, April 18, 1862.

The PRESIDENT *pro tempore.* If there be no morning business, the Chair will call up the unfinished business of yesterday, which is a bill (S. No. 75) to establish a Line of Steam Mail Ships between San Francisco, in California, and Shanghae, in China, touching at the Sandwich Islands and Japan; on which the Senator from California has the floor.

Mr. LATHAM. That may lie over for a little while, until there is a quorum. There is evidently not a quorum here now. I want to press the measure to a vote. No doubt the committee rooms are filled. There are two or three committees in session this morning, to my knowledge.

The PRESIDENT *pro tempore.* Does the Senator make a motion?

Mr. LATHAM. Let it go over informally. I will call it up again.

The PRESIDENT *pro tempore.* It will lie on the table for the present.

* * * * * * * * * * *

STEAMSHIP LINE TO CHINA.

Mr. LATHAM. I now move that the Senate proceed to the consideration of Senate bill No. 75.

The motion was agreed to, and the Senate, as in Committee of the Whole, resumed the consideration of the bill (S. No. 75) to establish a Line of Steam Mail Ships between San Francisco, in California, and Shanghae, in China, touching at the Sandwich Islands and Japan.

The PRESIDENT *pro tempore.* Upon this question the Senator from California is entitled to the floor.

Mr. LATHAM. I have nothing to say upon the subject in addition to what I stated the other day, with the exception of a fact that I wish to present to the Senate in consequence of objections that I know exist in the minds of many Senators with whom I have conversed in relation to this bill.

The PRESIDENT *pro tempore.* The Chair desires further to state, that the question pending is on the amendment moved by the Senator from California to strike out all of the original bill, after the enacting clause, and to insert a substitute.

Mr. SUMNER. The Senator from California knows very well I take a sincere interest in his bill, and I listened with great attention to the able and elaborate speech in which he developed his idea. It seems to me that if it can be carried out, it cannot do otherwise than great good to our commerce; but the Senator himself did confess to a considerable expenditure which would be entailed upon the country if the system were attempted. The point to which I wish to bring his attention, if he will allow me, is to what extent that expenditure can be made consistent with the present condition of things, and with the extraordinary expenditures to which our Treasury is exposed; in other words, whether, at this moment, when we are engaged in this extraordinary war, we can, with proper reference to the finances of the country, assume this additional burden. If we were in a moment of peace, if we had no extraordinary expenditures, then I should feel constrained by the argument of the Senator. The difficulty with me is that we are not in a condition to assume any new and extraordinary expenses.

The PRESIDENT *pro tempore.* The question is on the amendment offered by the Senator from California.

Mr. FESSENDEN. I should like to hear the amendment read.

The Secretary read it, to strike out all of the original bill after the enacting clause, and insert:

That the Postmaster-General be, and hereby is authorized and directed to enter into a contract, for a term not exceeding five years, for a sum not exceeding $500,000 per annum, with such person or persons, being the lowest bidders, offering sufficient and satisfactory security, after due public notice, for the transportation of the United States mails, upon the best terms for the United States, monthly, and in thirty-five days, from San Francisco, California, via the Sandwich Islands and Japan, in case any port of that empire shall be opened to the United States, to Shanghae, in China, and back, in steam vessels of not less than two thousand tons burden, of the best form of construction adapted to the navigation of the Pacific ocean; and any excess of the amount which may be contracted to be paid for this service over the aggregate of postages collected therefor, shall be paid out of any money in the Treasury not otherwise appropriated.

SEC. 2. *And be it further enacted,* That these mail steam vessels shall be appropriately armed and equipped as war steamers, in such manner as the Secretary of the Navy may direct; they shall each be commanded by a lieutenant of the United States Navy, and while employed in carrying the mails, as herein provided, they shall be required to protect commerce in their route between Shanghae and San Francisco, in the same manner as if the said vessels were wholly devoted to that service.

Mr. LATHAM. Mr. President, I think I can answer successfully the objection made by the honorable Senator from Massachusetts to this bill. I know very well, as I stated the other day, that a proposition of this kind ought not, in the present condition of affairs, to be made, unless for good and sufficient reasons. I am prepared to show to the Senate that the protection given by our Government to the commerce of the Pacific coast is wholly inadequate to the interests involved; in the next place, to show, that if the Government pursues the policy indicated in this bill it will be really an economy; and in the third place, that the interests of our country there, are such that they will suffer to a very alarming extent unless we go to the expense of increasing the Navy on the one hand, or of adopting a system like this on the other.

In the first place, on the Pacific coast we have but six men-of-war. The Navy Register shows that the Pacific squadron consists of the Lancaster, 26 guns; steam sloop Saranac, 9 guns; sloop St. Mary's, 22 guns; the steam sloop Wyoming, 6 guns; the steam sloop Narragansett, 5 guns; and the sloop Cyane, 20 guns. There are four steam sloops out of the six vessels that are in all the Pacific waters. These ships are principally stationed in the large harbors which line the coast extending from Chili up to the British possessions in the North-west. The flag-ship Lancaster is located almost permanently, I may say, in the bay of Panama, for the purpose of protecting the commerce that we have monthly between the Atlantic and the Pacific coasts. The sloop Cyane is located almost permanently in the harbor of Acapulco, because our position with the Mexican Government is such that some vessel of war is imperative at that place, to protect our commerce and preserve amicable relations. The other vessels, with the exception of one, are on the coast of South America; so that now our trade with the East Indies and with the Chinese ports, since the misfortune that happened to the steamship known as the Saginaw very recently, is entirely without a single vessel to protect them. There is not a single armed vessel carrying the American flag in all those waters.

As against this showing, the British Government have got in those northern waters—not in the southern Pacific, but in the northern Pacific—a long list of men-of-war, which I beg the attention of the Senate in reading, as follows:

| | *Guns.* | *Tonnage.* | *H. P.* |
|---|---|---|---|
| Steam flag-ship Bacchante | 51 | 2,667 | 600 |
| Steam sloop Cameleon | 17 | 952 | 200 |
| Steam corvette Clio | 22 | 1,472 | 400 |
| Steam sloop Fawn | 17 | 751 | 100 |
| Steam sloop Harrier | 17 | 748 | 100 |
| Paddle sloop Hecate | 6 | 817 | 240 |
| Steam sloop Miranda | 15 | 1,039 | 250 |
| Steam sloop Mutine | 17 | 882 | 200 |
| Storeship Naiad | 6 | 1,020 | ...... |
| Storeship Nereus | 6 | 1,094 | ...... |
| Steam corvette Pelorus | 21 | 1,462 | 400 |
| Steam corvette Tartar | 20 | 1,296 | 250 |
| Steam frigate Termagant | 25 | 1,547 | 310 |
| Steam frigate Topaze | 51 | 1,973 | 600 |
| Gunboat Forward | ... | ....... | 60 |
| Gunboat Grappler | ... | ....... | 60 |
| Total (16 ships) | 291 | 17,729 | 3,770 |

The French Government in the same quarter have the following fleet to protect their commerce, which is of a very limited character as compared with our own:

| | *Guns.* | *Men.* | *H. P.* |
|---|---|---|---|
| Steam flag-ship Duguay Trouin | 90 | 1,000 | 800 |
| Corvette Galathee | 32 | 300 | ...... |
| Corvette Cornelie | 32 | 300 | ...... |
| Corvette Bayonnaise | 32 | 300 | ...... |
| Screw steamer Oassini | 6 | 180 | 250 |
| Total | 102 | 3,080 | 1,050 |

Both these Governments have recently increased their force in those waters. During the time when there was a difficulty pending, growing out of the Trent affair, additional vessels were ordered by both of those Governments into the Pacific waters. The number I am unable to state, because I have no means of knowing.

I wish now to present to the Senate an estimate from the Navy Department as to the cost of maintaining those vessels on the Pacific station. I will take the Lancaster, which, as I have stated, is located in the bay of Panama, as an illustration. The annual expense to the Government of maintaining the Lancaster is $405,414 per annum. The pay of officers, marines and seamen amounts to $97,374; provisions, $35,040; wear and tear and consumption of stores, $84,000; and fuel per annum, $189,000; making a total of $405,414. Three such ships as is contemplated by this bill, and for which we ask but a subsidy of $500,000, would cost the Government annually $1,216,242. Three such vessels as the little St.

Mary's, a mere sloop, a sailing vessel, would amount per annum to $299,823. Three such vessels as the Cyane, another sailing vessel, would amount to $266,280 per annum. The payment of officers, marines and seamen in each is estimated at nearly sixty thousand dollars per annum; provisions $20,000; and the wear and tear and consumption of stores, between twenty and thirty thousand dollars; so that, if you take three of these vessels, mere sloops, the charge made in this bill would really be economical on the part of the Government.

Senators whose attention has not been called specifically to this question may not be aware of the extent of our commerce in those waters; they may not know what amount of property we have there. Why, sir, a work that I have been able to get hold of, published a few years ago, shows that the American trading vessels in the Pacific alone amount to 650, with a tonnage of 200,000, and with 16,000 men employed. The vessels engaged in the American whale fisheries which would, necessarily, be incidentally protected by vessels traversing the route prescribed in this bill in the Pacific waters amount to 634, with a tonnage of 223,109, and employing 18,000 men. Their value is $30,000,000, and give us a yearly profit of $10,000,000. The total number of vessels in the Pacific that are to be protected incidentally by these steamers, as provided for in this bill, amount to 1,284, with a tonnage of 423,109, and with 34,000 navigators, and a total value of $70,000,000. This was an estimate made several years ago, which must now be necessarily much increased. I have been unable to obtain a very recent estimate, but I state the above as reliable.

Mr. President, I consumed so much of the time of the Senate the other day on this question, that I did not, as I might have done, allude to these statistics so elaborately. Senators may naturally ask why should we engage in a trade of this kind, supposing our commercial relations with that Government are not of a character to justify us in this outlay. Why, sir, with the exception of the European trade, there is no part of the known habitable globe with whom our commercial relations are so extensive, or have been so growing, as with the Chinese empire. Let me take one article alone—the article of tea. I make no allusion to the silks, to the works of art, to the dye-stuffs, and to other commodities that we import from that country; but I choose to take that article which is best known to Senators and the country, and call your attention to the trade in that article. I will read, for instance, the relative trade between England and our country in the article of tea.

"In the first half of this time, that is, from 1792 to 1822, England imported of tea from China 737,637,740 pounds, or an average of 24,587,591 pounds per year. The total value of her trade with that country, in this period, was $1,894,813,474, or an annual trade of $63,160,449, and from which the Government of Great Britain derived in this period the aggregate *revenue* of $440,233,422. In the succeeding thirty years, that is, from 1822 to 1852, the quantity of tea imported by England reached the aggregate weight of 1,208,045,-111 pounds, or an annual average of 40,268,170 pounds. At the beginning of the term, the yearly import was about 23,000,000 pounds, and it now averages about 54,000,000 pounds annually. In this last thirty years, the English derived in duties from this tea trade alone $550,311,614, or a yearly revenue of $18,343,720.

"The first voyage from the United States to China was made in 1785, but the trade was not fairly opened until 1792; from that period it has continued to increase until our importations of teas now average about 16,000,000 pounds annually. The total value of imports from the commencement of the trade to this time has reached the amount of $258,-858,283. Our exports have amounted to $86,260,264; leaving to be paid in the precious metals $172,598,019."

The reason why the balance of trade is against us is because the specie carrying business that was done by our Government alone up to 1827, has been entirely taken by the English, as I explained to the Senate the other day. Up to 1827, our vessels had carried direct to China the sum of $88,851,606. The opium trade sprang up as between the British East Indies and the Chinese ports about that time, so that the balance of trade was in favor of England; and in order to meet that, as I stated the other day, our American bills of credit were substituted for the specie carrying trade. The result has been that, from 1827 down to 1834, the specie that we sent to China amounted only to $7,988,616, while our American bills on Chinese account payable in London, for the same time, amounted to $16,657,476.

The PRESIDENT *pro tempore.* The Senator from California will suspend his remarks. The hour has arrived for the consideration of the special order of the day, which, by force of the rules, supersedes the consideration of the present bill. The bill now before the Senate, therefore, is Senate bill No. 151, to confiscate the property and free the slaves of rebels.

Mr. HOWARD. I will state to the Senate that I desire to make some observations on that bill, and would be glad to proceed now, unless it will interfere seriously with the measure which is before the Senate, advocated by my friend from California.

The PRESIDENT *pro tempore.* The Senator from Michigan is entitled to the floor.

Mr. LATHAM. With the permission of the Senator from Michigan, I should like to finish this bill. It will not occupy a long time. I am nearly through. I do not think it willl give rise to any discussion.

Mr. HOWARD. Then I will yield for that purpose.

Mr. LATHAM. I should like very much to have the bill finished to-day.

Mr. FESSENDEN. I can only say that the disscussion will not end probably with the remarks of the honorable Senator from California. I shall have a word or two to say upon this measure; they will not be long, to be sure; and I do not know what other Senators may desire to speak. I cannot allow it to pass without entering my protest against it, to say the least of it.

The PRESIDENT *pro tempore.* The floor is at the disposition of the Senator from Michigan.

Mr. HOWARD. If that be the case, I will proceed.

* * * * * * * * * *

* * * * * * * * * *

Mr. LATHAM. After the wish expressed by the honorable Senator from Kentucky, I move that the Senate proceed to the consideration of the unfinished business of the morning hour, which was laid aside in order to take up the special order, on which the Senator from Michigan has spoken.

The PRESIDENT *pro tempore.* If it be the pleasure of the Senate the bill now under consideration, the confiscation bill, will be passed over, remaining as the unfinished business of the day, and the Senate will proceed to the consideration of the bill on which the Senator from California had the floor, which the special order interrupted. If there be no objection, the bill will be considered as before the Senate. The Chair hears no objection.

The Senate, as in Committee of the Whole, resumed the consideration of the bill (S. No. 75) to establish a Line of Steam Mail Ships between San Francisco, in California, and Shanghae, in China, touching at the Sandwich Islands and Japan.

Mr. LATHAM. I had nearly concluded what I had to say to the Senate when the special order interrupted me. I was showing the influence that had been exerted by the English through the means of the opium trade in diverting the course of specie sent from our country to Chinese traders, and I had just called attention to the fact that from 1827 to 1834 our specie sent to China direct amounted only to a little over seven millions of dollars, while the American bills payable in London since that time to cover the balances found due had swelled up to the enormous amount of $75,757,797. I was about to say that this is an unnatural course of trade, for the reason that our country produces the very same things for consumption that the British does; we manufacture the same articles; and there is no reason whatever why our people should not avail themselves of their market instead. We are more in contact, nearer of approach, and more able to compete for that trade than any other nation on the face of the earth.

Let me take the exports for one year from the two countries, Great Britain and our own, from which the Senate will be able to see their relative proportions and discrepancies:

EXPORTS FROM ENGLAND TO CHINA.

| *Cotton Goods.* | | |
|---|---|---|
| Unbleached muslins | 1,792,321 | pieces. |
| Bleached muslins | 645,356 | " |
| Twilled cottons | 133,591 | " |
| Calicoes or chintzes | 75,174 | " |
| Cotton handkerchiefs | 61,480 | dozen. |
| Cotton yarn | 4,314,947 | lbs. |
| *Woolen Goods.* | | |
| Broad cloths | 334,643 | pieces. |
| Cassimeres | 303,717 | " |
| Camlets | 381,773 | " |
| Blankets | 6,335 | pairs. |

EXPORTS FROM UNITED STATES TO CHINA.

| *Cotton Goods.* | | |
|---|---|---|
| Unbleached muslins | 90,523 | pieces. |
| Bleached muslins | 6,398 | " |
| Twilled cottons | 116,140 | " |
| Calicoes or chintzes | 3,130 | " |
| Cotton handkerchiefs | 250 | dozen. |
| Cotton yarn | 59,567 | lbs. |
| *Woolen Goods.* | | |
| Broad cloths | 615 | pieces. |
| Cassimeres | 968 | " |
| Camlets | 4,958 | " |
| Blankets | none. | |

We have here the staple article, can manufacture as cheap, if not cheaper, than England, the expense of transportation quite as small, and there is no reason in the world why this marked difference should exist. This trade is ours by all laws of geography, and we should not permit it to pass from our hands.

But to return to the objection of the Senator from Massachusetts, I feel perfectly authorized in saying, and I believe in so doing I express the wish of my constituency, that if Congress would pass this bill and give our commence the protection these steamers would afford, traveling monthly throughout the entire Northern Pacific, it can withdraw every vessel it has now in the Northern Pacific, costing the Government at present between one and two millions of dollars. I do not mean to disparage the efforts and energies of our ships-of-war stationed on the Pacific coast, for I believe they do all they can, but they are of little, if any, protection to the whaling trade or to the American trade that is engaged in our Northern Pacific. Why, sir, of what benefit, except for that isolated and local protection, is the stationing of the Cyane in the bay of Acapulco, or the Lancaster in the bay o Panama? None whatever. If an outrage is committed, or a wrong of any kind inflicted by any foreign Government, before we could get redress a long time must elapse, besides trusting to the uncertainties of negotiation and diplomacy. Once give us a line like this, constituting the militia of the seas, traveling periodically from San Francisco to the Sandwich Islands, to Japan, and to China, and it would be of more benefit and more protection to our commerce than all the vessels now located in the whole Pacific, both Northern and Southern. Having shown you that the Lancaster alone costs nearly half a million annually, the whole subsidy we ask for this entire line; and if economy is your object, after giving us this, take away your war vessels, and place them where they may be of greater service to the country.

Mr. President, this is a measure which the constituency I represent have very much at heart. It occupies the attention of the commercial people of that coast more than any other, except the great Pacific railroad. It has been asked for not only by our Legislature and by our Chamber of Commerce, but by repeated petitions, praying that this commerce given to us by nature, shall not pass forever from us. I know the belief on the part of some is that the State itself is perfectly able to take care of itself; but it strikes me that any such idea is a very contracted one. If you intend to put these remote portions of the country on their proper basis as a portion of the Union, you must give them equal and necessary assistance as well as protection from foreign aggression. Why, sir, I hold in my hand a table of the annual gold productions of the State of California, a large proportion of which, as I endeavored to show the other day, would have long since found its way across the Pacific by this proposed means, had Congress seen fit to establish it, enriching us, instead of foreign countries.

The table shows that during the short time of our existence, from 1849 down to the present period, the yield of gold in that State has amounted to over seven hundred and seventy-one millions of dollars, as follows:

*Table exhibiting the Shipment of Treasure from San Francisco to 31st December,* 1860 *to all quarters, and also to New York; the receipts of gold at the United States Mint and branches, and the estimated yield of the mines of California, since* 1848.

| Year. | Shipments to all quarters as manifested. | Shipments to New York. | Receipts at Mint and branches. | Estimated yield of California. |
|---|---|---|---|---|
| 1848.......... | ........................ | ........................ | ........................ | $ 60.000 |
| 1849.......... | $ 4,921,250 | ........................ | $ 5,232.249 | 8,000,000 |
| 1850.......... | 27,676.346 | ........................ | 28,206,226 | 33,000,000 |
| 1851.......... | 45,582.695 | ........................ | 57,138.980 | 55,000,000 |
| 1852.......... | 46,586,134 | ........................ | 51,470,675 | 57,000,000 |
| 1853.......... | 57,331,024 | $47.916,448 | 62,838.395 | 69,000,000 |
| 1854.......... | 51,328,653 | 46,289,649 | 46,719,083 | 64.000,000 |
| 1855.......... | 43,080,211 | 38.730,564 | 47,419,945 | 65,000.000 |
| 1856.......... | 48,887,543 | 39,765.294 | 56,379.901 | 70,000.000 |
| 1857.......... | 48.592.743 | 35,287,778 | 55,217.843 | 70,000,000 |
| 1858.......... | 47.548,025 | 35,578,236 | 51.494,311 | 70,000,000 |
| 1859.......... | 47,640,463 | 39,831,937 | 52,000,000 | 70,000.000 |
| 1860.......... | 42,325,916 | 35,665,500 | 27,037,919 | 70.000,000 |
| 1861.......... | ........................ | ........................ | ........................ | 70 000,000 |
| | Total......... | ........................ | ........................ | $771,060,000 |

Not long since a memorial, bearing date of December 5, 1861, was presented from the Chamber of Commerce of the city of New York, in which I find the following statement:

"To all the considerations before mentioned may be added the fact that the foreign commerce of the State of New York has increased, since the first export of California gold at this port, about *two hundred per cent.*"

In 1849 the imports of that port (New York city) were $92,567,369; the exports $45,963,100; making a total of $138,530,469.

In 1860 the imports were $248,489,877; the exports $145,555,449; making a total of $394,045,326, or an increase during the time these shipments of gold had continued, of $255,514,857.

Feeling loth to occupy any more time of the Senate, I shall now leave the matter in the hands of those who are best able to judge of the interests of the Government and of their sense of duty in the premises. Whatever may be the result of this bill, whether passed by the Senate or rejected, I can only feel that I have done my duty, and a pleasant one, in presenting and urging upon the consideration of this body all the facts available and patent within my reach that would in any way convince or favorably influence your judgments.

The PRESIDENT *pro tempore.* The question is on the amendment moved by the Senator from California.

Mr. FESSENDEN. I am not aware of the relative merits of the original bill and the amendment; I have heard the amendment read, but I do not know what the provisions of the bill are. I suppose, however, from the confidence I have in my friend from California, and his knowledge of the subject and general accuracy of views, that the amendment is undoubtedly an improvement upon the bill. But, sir, I am opposed to both of them at the present time; I am opposed to the thing whatever shape it may assume. I am disposed to be liberal in my votes on all these matters, and have been heretofore, and I do not know but what under another state of things in the country I should be desposed to give my support to this object on looking into it and being satisfied that the good effects might be likely to flow from it which are supposed by the Senator from California. But the Senate is aware and the country is aware that we have heretofore, in the period of our legislation, adopted, to a certain extent, this system of subsidizing steamers, paying subsidies in the shape of postal arrangements in order to facilitate and increase trade. I do not know but that the object is a legitimate one. It was, at all events, one that recommended itself to Congress and was tried; but the Senate must be equally aware that after a trial of that system for several years, it was deliberately laid aside and abandoned by Congress, at a period, too, when the country was in a high state of prosperity, its finances entirely unembarrassed, and when we were perfectly able to undertake such a system and carry it on. Perhaps it was unwise to abandon it.

One would think, however, that if it was to be recommenced, it should be recommenced where our trade is the largest and most direct, and especially with reference to postages where it would be likely to yield something like a return. We must be aware that this being established under the Post Office Department, amounts to nothing and can amount to nothing comparatively; it is a mere cover for the greater object, the ulterior object, of promoting and protecting trade. I am a friend to that, and at a proper time and under proper circumstances I should be willing to avail myself of any provision of the Constitution which would enable me to accomplish that purpose reasonably; but at the present time I am averse to any of these undertakings which are matters of experiment alone, although there are the fairest prospects that the experiment will succeed; and I am opposed to it simply for the reason that we have on our hands now an undertaking which will tax our resources to the utmost, and is doing so at the present time. We have a large amount of debt unpaid; we are put to the use of all our energies, of all our capabilities, to get along with that which is absolutely pressing upon us as a necessity.

Now, however favorable I might be to this object, and however willing I may be—and certainly nobody has shown himself more so by his votes than I have—to advance the interests of our friends upon the Pacific coast by every legitimate means in the world, even for them I am unwilling to devote such large sums of money to undertakings of this description. I think that our friends there, as well as in other parts of the country, can afford to wait for a short period of time until the country shall be able to resume its original position, and be able to appropriate something for this purpose.

I will not go into a review of any portion of the argument of the honorable Senator. I think some of his suggestions can be readily met and answered, while others it might be more difficult to manage. Leaving all that out of the question, I must call the attention of the Senate to the fact that it is as much as we can possibly do with the necessities on hand to meet the obligations of the Government; and I do not think we should be held excusable at the present time for returning again to a system or an undertaking which leads to a system that was once commenced, and was, in days of prosperity, deliberately abandoned. I may not have agreed with the policy of abandoning that system at the time we did, and in the manner we did; but if those times had been these, if we were then in the same position that we are now, I should have had no doubt that this was a proper point at which we could save the expenditure of money. I trust the time is not far distant when the resources of the country will enable us to return to any system that has been found beneficial, or that we may judge beneficial hereafter; but I think that our friends on the Pacific are pressing a little too hard when they tell us that measures like this, which we agree, those matters important to themselves in which we may think alike, and which we may be disposed to encourage and sustain at the earliest possible opportunity, should be pressed and undertaken at a moment like this.

That is my general view of the subject, and, for my own part, I am unwilling to consider any proposition of this description having reference to improvements and facilities in trade, and other matters of which we are all unquestionably in favor, that can be postponed without material injury. I admit the existence of the truth that a nation must depend for its ability to support itself in war, in a time of great expenditure, upon its resources, upon trade and commerce, and the other great sources of national wealth; but we cannot originate them in time of war; they must be originated in time of peace. This is no time to take out of the Treasury money which we have not, if I may so express myself; money which is absolutely essential for our daily expenditures, and which cannot be dispensed with for those purposes, and apply it to untried experiments, much less to experiments which have been tried and failed, so far as revenue was concerned. As a member of the Committee on Finance, and having more particularly in view the resources of the country with reference to meeting what we must meet daily, I feel it my duty to place this simple and single view of the subject before Congress in reference to this bill and all other bills of a similar description.

Mr. McDOUGALL. Mr. President, I did not expect to engage in this discussion now. I hoped, however, to have a time when I might say a few words that, I think, may have some value. I should like to discourse on this and kindred subjects somewhat at length at some other time. Now, however, I shall say a few words. I have not felt it incumbent on me to present the peculiar considerations that belong to this question, for it has been taken charge of, so far as my State is concerned, by my colleague, and I know him to be a man of eminent ability; and after having heard and read his discourse on the subject, I felt satisfied that the general aspects of the question had been presented admirably, and that I could not improve them.

But, sir, there is one view of the subject which I propose to discuss now briefly, wherein I differ radically from the Senator from Maine; and I get my wisdom from the teachings of past history. What I have to say now is rather for suggestion than for advice. Sir, we are talking about economical measures, not about developing the country; we are talking about economical measures; not about administrative policy; we are talking about non-action, not of action; and therein we are guilty of a great want of wisdom, in my judgment. After England had been involved in the wars that grew out of the French revolution, and great debts were charged upon her, there was this cry that I hear from the Senator from Maine. The great debt of the country, the great debt that is being accumulated upon our shoulders, is now spoken of here. So it was there. And when the persons who were seeking popular favor sought to alarm the people of England, the greatest man in modern times in the British Parliament, in responding to the cry of the oppression of debt and of taxation, said something like this: "but for these wars and this great burden, our ships would not have been upon all the seas; it has demanded from England the full expression of the strength of all her sons; it has developed her commerce with all the nations, and it has sent her ships upon every sea." I do not quote the language; I speak the substance of what was said by Fox in the English Parliament when they were talking about England being overwhelmed with £800,000,000 sterling of debt. Adversaries made England strong. We are not weak, and we are not hurt by these assaults. The masters of politico-economical science who undertake to say that because we happen to be in debt $1,500,000,000—I will assume that as the figure—therefore we, the people of this Republic, are in trouble—do not understand what are the resources of a great, free people. England represents a great, free people, next to ourselves, where the energies of the people are brought to bear to meet the necessities of the day, not by the nod of a monarch, but by action in Parliament.

Now, I have to say that we ought not to fear these things. Let us develop our national strength in every form, and not be afraid. We are still the North American Republic. We are still a Government which has power over every State from the Gulf of Mexico to the northern lakes, and from the shores of the Pacific to the shores of the Atlantic. The accidents of our condition are temporary. It is of the first importance that we should bind ourselves together, and not neglect to strengthen ourselves by compelling the wealth of other States. There is the East, and I call Senators' attention to it; and they who ignore it will find themselves in great fault. There is the wealth of the Orient, and what wealth is that? There are merchants in towns in China who could buy out any twenty merchants in the city of New York. It is a country full of wealth. Milton was not wrong when he talked about "barbaric pearls and gold." India, again, is the subject of a contest for command. By our position on the Pacific we have the opportunity to command all the ancient East; and if those who occupy high places of power refuse to lend the aid of the Government, by legislation and counsel, to promote these results, they will find that they have substitutes here at no very far period in the future.

Of all the questions that belong to the march of civilization and to the development of this country, wherein the extremest East is reproduced in the farthest West—of all these problems to them must belong, and to them must immediately relate two questions: one is steam communication between our possessions on the Pacific and the ancient East, and the other is iron communication between the shores of the Atlantic and the shores of the Pacific. These are the two great questions that belong to the age, and those who ignore them will be crushed under the iron wheels of the great car of progress.

Mr. POWELL. I move that the Senate adjourn.

Mr. LATHAM. I hope not.

Mr. FESSENDEN. Does the Senator imagine that he can get a vote on this bill to-day?

Mr. LATHAM. I want to get a vote on the amendment.

Mr. POWELL. I withdraw my motion.

The amendment was agreed to.

The bill was reported to the Senate; and the amendment was concurred in.

The PRESIDENT *pro tempore.* The question is on ordering the bill to be engrossed for a third reading.

Mr. FESSENDEN. On that question I ask for the yeas and nays.

The yeas and nays were ordered.

Mr. POWELL. Now I move that the Senate adjourn. There is evidently no quorum here.

The motion was agreed to; and the Senate adjourned.

* * * * * * * * * *

* * * * * * * * * *

## IN SENATE.

FRIDAY, April 25, 1862.

* * * * * * * * * *

The hour of half-past twelve o'clock having arrived, the special order for that hour was called up, and the Senate resumed the consideration of the bill (S. No. 75) to establish a Line of Steam Mail Ships between San Francisco, in California, and Shanghae, in China, touching at the Sandwich Islands and Japan.

Mr. COLLAMER. When this bill was up the other day, I suggested that a vote should not then be taken. I had heard other gentlemen say they desired to speak upon it. I have no wish to speak upon it. I will merely say that I doubt the propriety of again establishing a policy of this kind in the present condition of our country.

Mr. GRIMES. I move to amend the second section of the bill by striking out the words "they shall each be commanded by a lieutenant of the United States Navy."

Mr. LATHAM. I have no objection to the amendment.

The amendment was agreed to.

Mr. HALE. I feel constrained to say a word or two on this subject, inasmuch as the bill was referred to the Committee on Naval Affairs, and the committee reported against the bill at this time. The committee did not go into an examination of the matter in regard to its relation to commerce and the postal facilities which this line will furnish to the country; but taking that view of it which made the reference of it to the Naval Committee appropriate, they thought that it was not expedient at the present time to recommend the passage of such a bill. The second section, it will be seen, is the one that refers to that matter; and it provides:

"That these mail steam vessels shall be appropriately armed and equipped as war steamers, in such manner as the Secretary of the Navy may direct; they shall each be commanded by a lieutenant of the United States Navy,"—

which latter clause has been stricken out—

"and while employed in carrying the mails, as herein provided, they shall be required to protect commerce in their route between Shanghae and San Francisco, in the same manner as if the said vessels were wholly devoted to that service."

I need not say that since this bill was first introduced, events which are familiar to all the Senate have produced as total a revolution in regard to the subject of naval warfare by steam vessels as ever has been known in any department of government from the foundation of the world, and what might have been considered appropriate and requisite and proper three months ago, would be considered, perhaps, as absurd at the present time. The committee did not, as I said at the outset, deem it their duty to inquire particularly in reference to the commercial or the postal relations which this line of steamers was to have to the interests of the country, but simply in regard to this latter subject; and the committee believed that in that connection it was not worthy the support of Congress. They came to that conclusion before the revolution of which I have spoken in public sentiment had occurred. Since that has occurred, it seems to me that all the reasons which influenced the committee in their decision are infinitely stronger than they were before, and that the attention of the Navy Department in this hour of the country's emergency and in this crisis of naval warfare, its energies and resources, should not be directed in any manner to the construction of vessels of this character. It was for these reasons that the committee were opposed to the adoption of this system then, and are opposed to it as such now.

The PRESIDENT *pro tempore.* The question is on ordering the bill to be engrossed for a third reading.

The question being taken by yeas and nays, resulted—yeas 27, nays 13, as follows:

YEAS—Messrs. Anthony, Browning, Carlile, Cowan, Davis, Doolittle, Henderson, Howard, Lane of Indiana, Lane of Kansas, Latham, McDougall, Nesmith, Pomeroy, Powell, Rice, Saulsbury, Simmons, Stark, Sumner, Thomson, Wade, Wilkinson, Willey, Wilson of Massachusetts, Wilson of Missouri, and Wright—27.

NAYS—Messrs. Chandler, Collamer, Dixon, Fessenden, Foot, Foster, Grimes, Hale, Howe, King, Morrill, Sherman, and Wilmot—13.

The bill was read a third time.

The PRESIDENT *pro tempore.* The question is, "Shall the bill pass?"

Mr. FESSENDEN. I ask for the yeas and nays upon the passage of the bill. It may be considered a very impertinent remark, but I must say that I can hardly suppose the Senate understood, especially the members of the Finance Committee, what they were voting for. This bill, in the present stage of our finances, makes a positive requisition upon the Government, not only authorizes, but directs, the Government to pay $500,000 a year to establish a line of steamships under the Post Office regulations, at a period when we need all the money we can get by any possibility to carry on the war, and when it is not to be supposed that any income whatever can come from it under the Post Office regulations. There is no Post Office business for this line to do; but it is to be established under the pretense of postal regulation, when we have abandoned that whole system on the Atlantic coast, where commerce, to a great extent, is carried, and where, if anywhere, we suffer from the competition of English steamers. The system has been tried and abandoned, and we have come to the plan of giving nothing whatever in the shape of subsidies except the postages. We abandoned the system which is now proposed to be again inaugurated after a deliberate trial, when our Treasury was full, when we had ample ability to sustain it; and yet, in this stage, where no postages and no income of any consequence at all can be expected under the Post Office regulations, it is proposed to establish this new line of steamships. I have said before, that a proper time, and when our Treasury could afford it, I might be in favor of the system; but at present I conceive it to be a matter that is fraught with very great danger.

I made all the remarks that I had to make upon it the other day, by way of argument and suggestion. If the Senate differ from me, I submit with all the grace that I can. I must do so; but I want it distinctly understood by everybody what the measure is. I cannot say that I am surprised at anybody's vote, because everybody else knows just as well as I do how to vote. I do not pretend to dispute that; but I am surprised at the members of my committee, who know what difficulty we have to get money, even for the current expenses of the day, voting in favor of this bill.

Mr. SIMMONS. I want to say one word in explanation of my vote. I know it has got to be somewhat of a habit for gentlemen to question the ability of the people to support the Government of the country. I have never entertained exactly the opinion of the chairman of the Committee on Finance about the deplorable condition of the finances of the country. I vote for this bill because I think its object a laudable one, that I would vote for at any time, that I have been in favor of for the last twenty years.

Mr. McDOUGALL. As the chairman of the Committee on Finance has stated his conclusions, and the chairman of the Committee on Naval Affairs has stated his, allow me to say that I have not discussed this question on the floor for the reason that I sought action and did not want to delay it; but I wish to say here that this is a measure not to take money out of, but to put money into the Federal Treasury; this is a measure not to weaken the strength of the Government, it is to give it strength. If there is any field of enterprise that demands the attention of the Federal Government, so that we may be strengthened in commercial relations, by finding a market for our manufactures, it is China at this present moment, and the time when we can seize an advantage should not be lost.

Mr. FESSENDEN. I ask for the yeas and nays on the passage of the bill.

The yeas and nays were ordered.

Mr. HALE. I voted in the minority and therefore cannot make a motion to reconsider; but if some gentleman who voted in the majority would move a reconsideration of the engrossment of the bill, I should like to submit another amendment to be acted upon.

Mr. WILKINSON. To accommodate the Senator from New Hampshire, I move to reconsider the vote ordering the bill to be engrossed for a third reading.

Mr. HALE. I will state to the Senate that my only object is to move an amendment to the bill.

Mr. McDOUGALL. Will the Senator state the amendment he desires to offer?

Mr. HALE. I will state it so that the Senate can vote understandingly on the motion to reconsider. I want to move an amendment to strike out the second section.

That is a naval matter entirely, and the views of the Naval Committee are that it is not worthy of the support of the Senate as a naval measure. If that is the opinion of the Naval Committee, to whom it appropriately belongs, it seems to me that the Senate should not fasten a naval measure on a postal bill. If it is a postal and commercial measure, let it stand on its own merits; do not saddle it on the Navy when the Navy do not ask it and do not w at. My amendment is simply to strike out the second section.

The PRESIDENT *pro tempore.* The Senator from Minnesota moves to reconsider the vote by which this bill was ordered to be engrossed for a third reading.

Mr. LATHAM. I hope the motion to reconsider will not prevail. The amendment suggested by the Senator from New Hamshire, if moved by him and adopted by the Senate, would emasculate the bill and render it in a great degree worthless for the purposes for which we wish the bill passed by the Senate.

Mr. GRIMES. If the motion of the Senator from Minnesota prevails, I shall propose to amend the bill by striking out the word "directed," in the fourth line of the first section, which makes it obligatory on the Postmaster General to expend this $500,000, leaving it with him to do it or not, as he may deem that the public interest will require, and there is where I think it ought to be left.

Mr. LATHAM. If I move to lay the motion to reconsider on the table, will it carry the bill with it?

The PRESIDENT *pro tempore.* It will carry the bill with it.

Mr. LATHAM. I shall not make the motion.

The motion to reconsider was not agreed to: there being on a division—ayes 17, noes 24.

The question being taken by yeas and nays on the passage of the bill, resulted—yeas 26, nays 16; as follows:

YEAS—Messrs. Anthony, Browning, Carlile, Cowan, Davis, Henderson, Howard, Lane of Indiana, Lane of Kansas, Latham, McDougall, Nesmith, Pomeroy, Powell, Rice, Saulsbury, Simmons, Stark, Sumner, Thomson, Wade, Wilkinson, Willey, Wilson of Massachusetts, Wilson of Missouri, and Wright—26.

NAYS—Messrs. Chandler, Clark, Collamer, Dixon, Fessenden, Foot, Foster, Grimes, Hale, Howe, King, Morrill, Sherman, Ten Eyck, Trumbull, and Wilmot—16.

So the bill was passed.

---

MURPHY & Co. *Printers, Booksellers and Stationers*, 182 *Baltimore street, Baltimore.*

www.ingramcontent.com/pod-product-compliance
Lightning Source LLC
LaVergne TN
LVHW011126110826
845150LV00008B/2262
* 9 7 8 1 4 1 8 1 9 5 5 2 6 *